AF504399

Missing Dad

Dear Dad,

I know you're no longer here, but I feel that I need to say this, even if it's just to honor the space you held in my life. Growing up without you was hard—there were times when I felt lost and confused, times when I needed your guidance and presence. But over the years, I've learned to forgive. I've come to realize that life is complicated, and even though you weren't there physically, I've found my own way forward.

I was born and raised in West Philadelphia, and through the challenges, I became an educator, entrepreneur, and youth leader. In a way, I've filled the void you left by stepping up to be a father figure for others who need one. In 2017, I started a nonprofit mentorship program called "Mentor Leaders Produce Mentor Leaders," where I help young men navigate the world and find their purpose, just like I had to do for myself. My mission is to raise awareness about the struggles young people face and to fight for equitable education and opportunities for those who are often overlooked. For the past 19 years, I've dedicated my life to teaching, mentoring, and leading. They call me Mr. G or Mr. Garrett, and I've built a community of young people who know that they have someone who believes in them.

Even though I didn't have you to guide me, I found strength within myself and used that strength to make a difference in others' lives. I want you to know that I carry no bitterness. I forgive you. I've grown into the man I needed to be, and I'm at peace with our story. In some way, I believe that you've always been a part of my journey, and I hope you're proud of the path I've taken.

With love and understanding,

Vincent

Caleb was skipping
happily as he walked home from school.
He had not felt this happy for a

time.
g
n
o
l

"Mom!"

Ma dukes
Mum Mum
Mommy
he shouted loudly as he opened the door.
He could not wait to share the great news
with her.
mama
ma
mother
mum
Mummy

"Over here!" his mom said from the kitchen.
"You'll never guess it, Mom!" Caleb cried,
running into the kitchen,

Edna
"Our award ceremony and move-up day is
next week.
And I have three awards!"

"Wow!" his mom said, pride filling her eyes. "Three awards! That's awesome!"

1 2 3

I'm so proud of you!

She hugged him tight and kissed him on the cheek.

The next few days passed by really quickly. Finally, it was the day before the award ceremony. That afternoon, Caleb suddenly remembered that his teacher had given them handouts about the dress code to share with their parents.

"I almost forgot about it!" Caleb said as he opened his backpack. The handout was still there, pressed between the pages of his science textbook.

Annual Awards Ceremony

Dress Code: Formal

He pulled it out and ran to look for his mom.

Caleb found his mom in the living room, reading a magazine. She looked up at the sound of his footsteps. She put down the magazine and looked at him with a puzzled look."What's the matter,Caleb?" she asked.

"Mom, I'm so sorry!" said Caleb, "I forgot that there was a dress code for the award ceremony!" He handed the flyer to his mom and gave her time to go through it.
"Oh, I see... " Mom said after reading the handout, "It says here that you have to wear a button-down shirt, pants, tie, and shoes."

"Yes, but the tie!" cried Caleb, "It says that we cannot wear clip-on ties!" Caleb had only worn clip-on ties so far and he had no idea how to properly tie a tie. He knew that he would need a lot of practice.

After getting back home, Caleb stood in front of the mirror and tried to tie the tie around his neck. Still, no matter how hard he tried, he could not do it. It kept getting tangled up in all possible ways!

"Argh!" Caleb yelled angrily as he pulled the tie away from his neck. It was really frustrating. Hearing him shout, his mom came to check on him. "This is not working!" Caleb cried, showing her the tie.

"Let me have a look," said his mom, "I watched some videos about tying a tie. Let's give it a go." And so, she tried to tie his tie for him. But she couldn't get the knot right. It always looked crooked.

"This is much more difficult than I thought..." Mom said, untying the tie for maybe the hundredth time. "Other boys have their dads to tie their ties!" Caleb yelled angrily, "It sucks to not have a dad!" Then, he stormed out of the room.

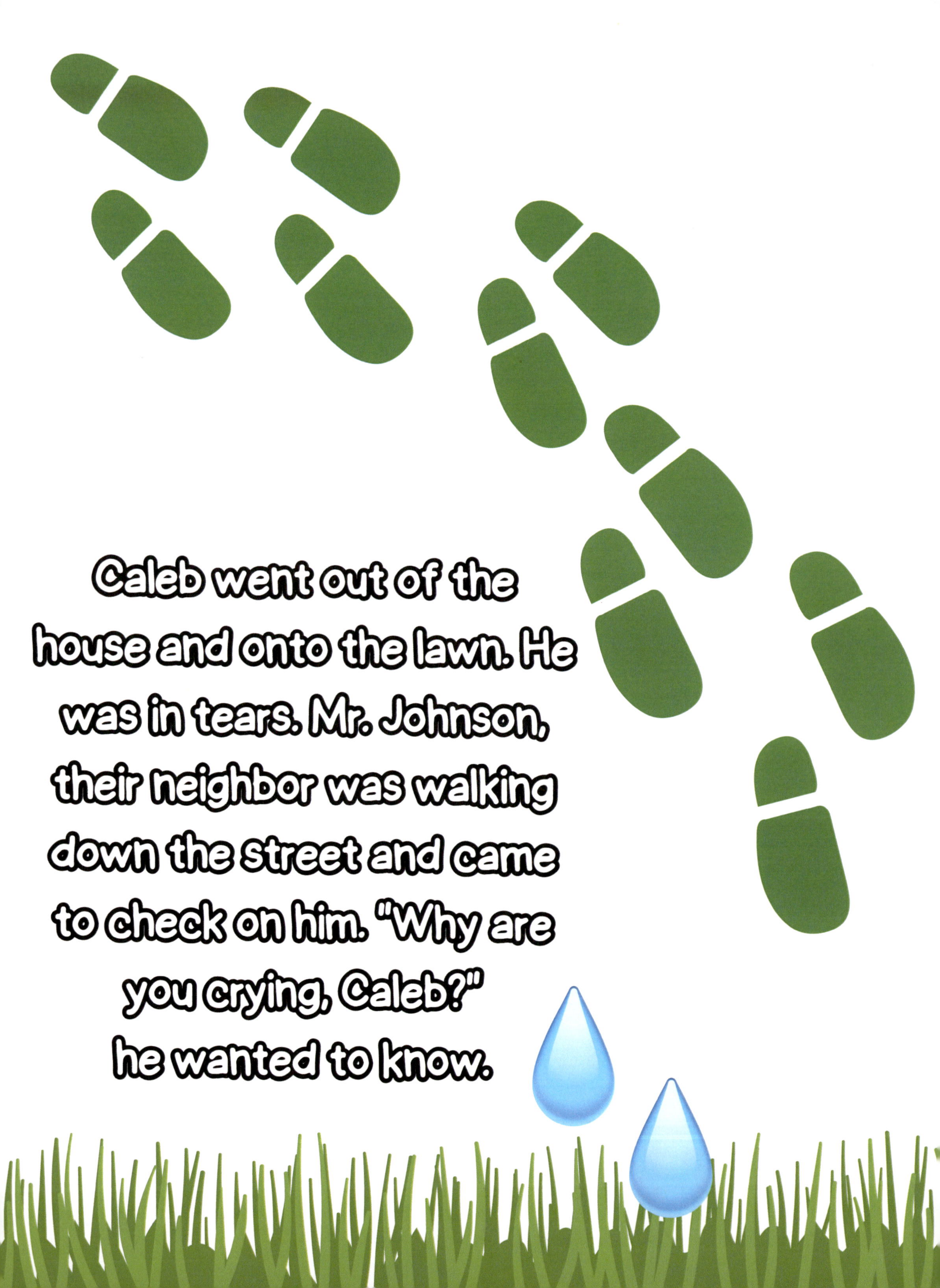

Caleb went out of the house and onto the lawn. He was in tears. Mr. Johnson, their neighbor was walking down the street and came to check on him. "Why are you crying, Caleb?" he wanted to know.

"I have to wear a tie tomorrow," Caleb told him, "But I don't know how to tie it by myself. I've tried many times but can't get it right. And I don't have a dad who can teach me. My mom has tried too, and couldn't get it either."

"How about I ask your mom if it's okay for you to come by my house tomorrow to help you tie it?" suggested Mr. Johnson,"I'll teach you how to tie a tie. And don't be so hard on your mom. She's doing everything she can for you." Caleb nodded tearfully .He knew what Mr. Johnson said was true and was thankful that he was willing to help him.

The next morning, Caleb put on his shirt, pants, and shoes and went to Mr. Johnson's house.

Mr.Johnson tied the tie for him. It took Mr. Johnson less than a minute and it looked perfect! Caleb smiled with happiness.
It felt GREAT to have a man to help him tie the tie.

Caleb and his mom headed to the school for the award's ceremony.

So many other kids were there with their parents. Almost all of them had their dads with them. Looking at them, Caleb began to feel emotional. He wished he was able to share that moment with his dad, whom he had never met.

When other kids climbed up the stage to get their awards, their dads cheered loudly for them.

"Way to go, my boy!"
"Go, Champ!"
"Well done, ace!
"Proud of you, my man!"

Each cheer made Caleb feel down. He thought that it was unfair that he didn't have a dad to cheer for him. When it was his turn to go up the stage, Caleb didn't even smile.
His heart was now heavy.

Next up is CALEB!!!,
who is on a roll collecting awards
like they're going
out of style!

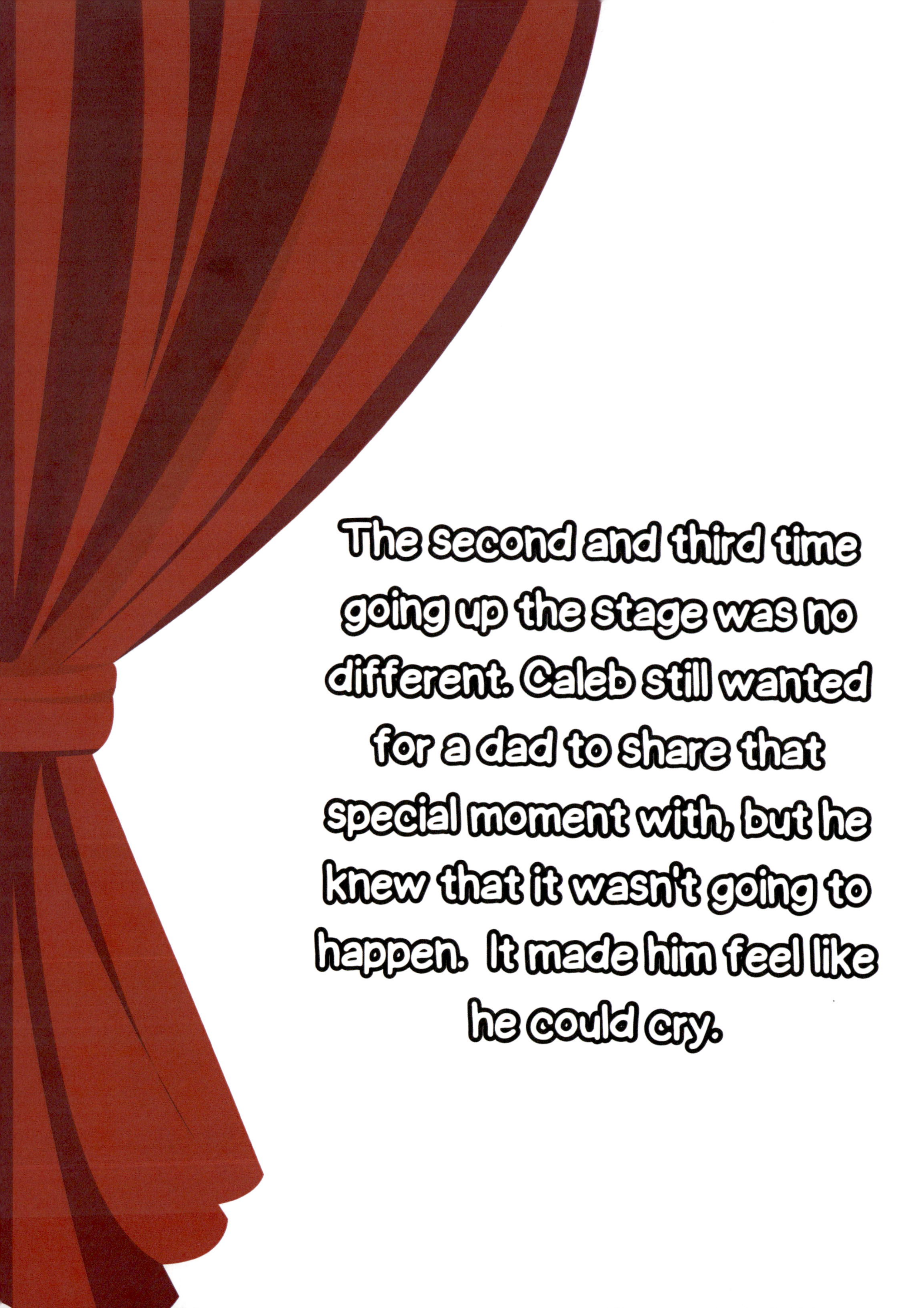

The second and third time going up the stage was no different. Caleb still wanted for a dad to share that special moment with, but he knew that it wasn't going to happen. It made him feel like he could cry.

But then, he looked up and saw his mom, sitting in the audience. She was beaming happily as if it was the best day of her life. She was so proud of him as she clapped and cheered for him.

"It's alright," Caleb thought to himself as he went down the stage and toward his mom, "My Mom is here, and she loves me

so much.

So, it's fine." But deep in his heart, he knew that having a dad would make all the difference. When his mom came over to him and hugged him, Caleb promised himself that he would not cry.

"I will be strong," he thought, hugging his mom back. "Even if I don't have a dad, I will try my best to be strong for both of us."

"Missing Dad" isn't just one book, it's a rollercoaster of 8 books packed with brain-teasing workbooks, vibrant coloring books, and action-packed activity books. Dive into our collection and join Caleb on more epic adventures! The 8 part series includes:

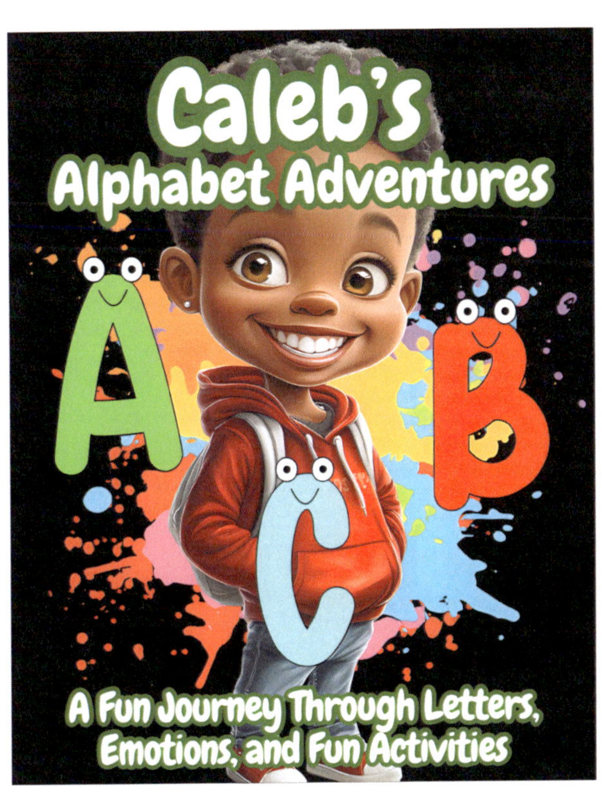

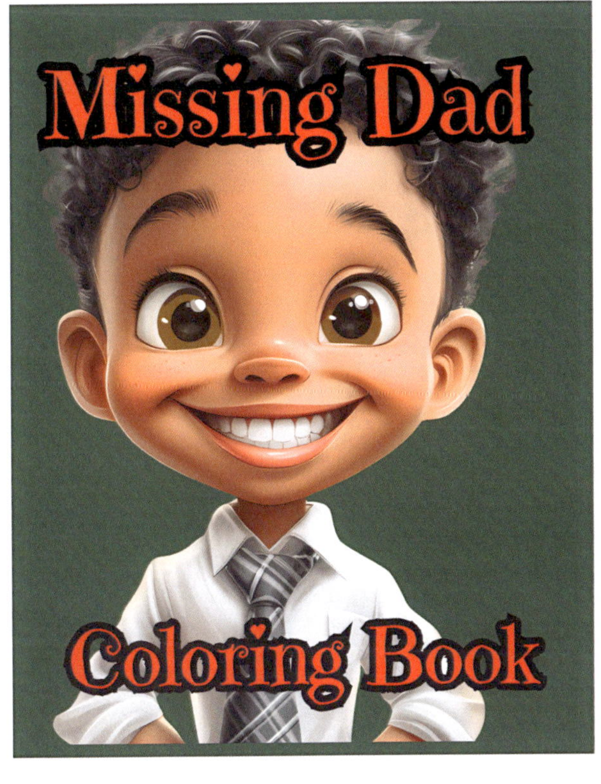

About The Author

Vincent Garrett was born and raised in West Philadelphia. He is a male educator, entrepreneur, youth leader, father, and father figure to many. He's also a community leader who advocates for the rights and well-being of young people. In April of 2017, Vincent started his nonprofit organization mentorship program for young men, "Mentor Leaders Produce Mentor Leaders" with the mission of raising awareness about social issues affecting youth, advocating for inclusive and equitable education, and working towards creating opportunities for underprivileged individuals in their community. Vincent, known as Mr. G or Mr. Garrett to his loving mentees, has been an educator for the past 19 years, dedicating his life to providing quality education to young people. He has worked as a teacher, a mentor, and an administrator, focusing on imparting knowledge, developing critical thinking skills, and fostering a love for learning in young minds. Overall, Vincent's passion for education, entrepreneurship, and community development is intended to make a lasting difference in the lives of young people and their communities.

www.ingramcontent.com/pod-product-compliance
Lightning Source LLC
Chambersburg PA
CBRC091646100726
47973CB00020B/253